Take
the Cake
You
Deserve
It!

Take the Cake

illustrations by
Linda Ketelhut

produced by
Smallwood & Stewart, Inc.

**Andrews McMeel
Publishing**

Kansas City

For information, write
Andrews McMeel Publishing,
an Andrews McMeel Universal company,
4520 Main Street, Kansas City, Missouri 64111.

ISBN: 0-7407-3867-4

Library of Congress Control Number:
2003103138

Produced by Smallwood & Stewart, Inc.
New York City

Illustrations by Linda Ketelhut
Designed by Curtis Potter

Wishes,
Wisdom,
and
Whimsy

BIRTHDAY · GIRL

(bûrth dä) (gûrl)

Person of exceptional **cuteness** who gets cooler every year.

VERY IMPORTANT BIRTHDAY GIRL

Here's to the girl who has everything:

SMARTS,
STYLE,
Looks, and
Fab Friends
(like me).

JANUARY
Famous Birthday Girls

6	Joan of Arc
7	Katie Couric
11	Naomi Judd
14	Faye Dunaway
17	Eartha Kitt
19	Dolly Parton
19	Janis Joplin
25	Virginia Woolf
29	Oprah Winfrey
31	Minnie Driver

Birthstone: Garnet

Garnet symbolizes swift movement. Act on a decision you've been putting off.

Insist on Your Birthday Upgrade All Day

ELITE STATUS

MEMBER: VIBG Numero Uno

SUNNIER

CHIC-ER

GREENER

TASTIER

SMILIER

BUBBLIER

STARRIER

IT'S A BIRTHDAY FACT!

1 Birthday girls are always right (that means you)!

2 Birthdays last an entire month.

3 If you karaoke on your birthday, you sound like a superstar.

4 Birthday workouts burn double the calories.

5 It's illegal to cry on your birthday.

FEBRUARY

Famous Birthday Girls

1   Lisa Marie Presley

2   Shakira

4   Rosa Parks

7   Laura Ingalls Wilder

11   Jennifer Aniston

12   Christina Ricci

18   Helen Gurley Brown

18   Yoko Ono

20   Cindy Crawford

27   Elizabeth Taylor

Birthstone: Amethyst

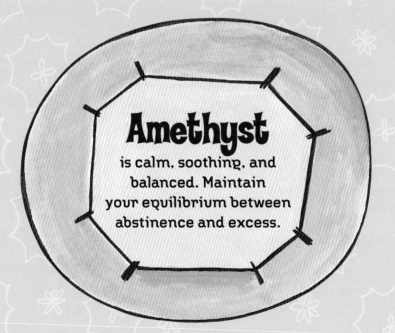

Amethyst is calm, soothing, and balanced. Maintain your equilibrium between abstinence and excess.

Be a Birthday Diva

Wear shades and a scarf all day – even indoors.

Give out autographs.

Call everyone "Darling" and use words like "Ciao," and "Bellissimo."

Travel with paparazzi and an entourage.

Carry a small dog.

Have a
High-Maintenance Day

TODAY YOUR MOOD RING READS

"HAPPY"

silly   flirty   girly   crazy   sassy

MARCH
Famous Birthday Girls

13 Charo
18 Queen Latifah
18 Vanessa Williams
25 Gloria Steinem
25 Aretha Franklin
26 Diana Ross
27 Mariah Carey
27 Sarah Vaughn
29 Elle Macpherson
30 Celine Dion

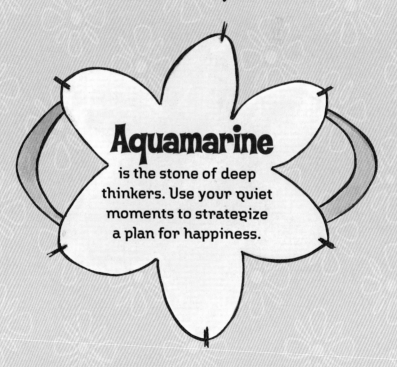

Aquamarine
is the stone of deep
thinkers. Use your quiet
moments to strategize
a plan for happiness.

Your Three Essential Birthday Rules

RULE #1

Treat yourself lightly.

Very Important Birthday Girl Spa
Purify
Pamper
tranquility
Energize
ESCAPE

RULE #2 Open the small presents first.

HAPPY BIRTHDAY HOUR TILL 8

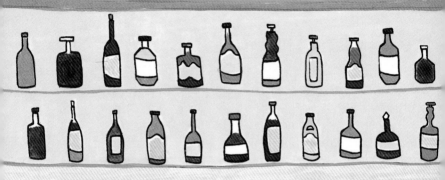

RULE
#3 *Throw yourself a big party.*

a toast to a Top-Shelf Day

APRIL

Famous Birthday Girls

3 Doris Day
5 Bette Davis
14 Sarah Michelle Gellar
17 Jennifer Garner
19 Ashley Judd
20 Jessica Lange
23 Shirley Temple
24 Barbra Streisand
25 Ella Fitzgerald
26 Carol Burnett

Birthstone: Diamond

Diamond

The crystal-clear stone
of a woman with goals.
Aim for the
ultimate prize

(which could be a
crystal-clear
diamond).

Here's to the
babe that's always
in fashion!

Sassy

Funky

Downtown

Uptown

Hip

Chic

Exchange your
personal baggage
for something
a little cuter.

MAY

Famous Birthday Girls

9   Candice Bergen
12 Katharine Hepburn
16 Janet Jackson
20 Cher
23 Joan Collins
22 Mary Cassatt
22 Naomi Campbell
24 Patti LaBelle
26 Peggy Lee
29 Melissa Etheridge

Emerald,

directs artistic ability.
Listen to the artisan
within and sign up for
that pottery class you've
been longing to take.

You're the only one
who is passionately
interested in your age;
other people have
their own troubles.

—Dorothy Parker,
U.S. writer, poet, and wit

The more you praise
and celebrate your life,
the more there is
in life to celebrate.

—Oprah Winfrey
U.S. talk-show host and actress

Your To-Do List

- ✓ *Follow your inner goddess.*
- ✓ *Get a rainbow pedicure.*
- ✓ *Buy a lot of shoes.*

the fun starts here

JUNE
Famous Birthday Girls

1	Marilyn Monroe
3	Josephine Baker
7	Anna Kournikova
8	Joan Rivers
13	Mary-Kate & Ashley Olsen
15	Courteney Cox
20	Nicole Kidman
22	Meryl Streep
25	Carly Simon
30	Lena Horne

Birthstone: Pearl

Pearl,
the seastone,
symbolizes dreams.
Expand your
dreams. There
is no limit!

Today's Forecast

A sunny, happy day with the chance
of a rose-petal shower in the afternoon,
followed by a beautiful starry night.
Outlook: Cool year ahead.

Women whose identity
depends more on their outsides
than their insides are dangerous
when they begin to age.

—Gloria Steinem,
U.S. feminist

. . .as soon as people
are old enough to know
better they don't
know anything at all.

—Oscar Wilde,
Irish wit, poet, and dramatist

JULY
Famous Birthday Girls

1	Liv Tyler
1	Missy Elliott
4	Ann Landers
6	Janet Leigh
9	Courtney Love
15	Linda Ronstadt
24	Jennifer Lopez
24	Amelia Earhart
28	Jacqueline Kennedy Onassis
31	J. K. Rowling

Birthstone: Ruby

Ruby has a deep red hue, which is the badge of courage. Take on the big things in life.

Dress up
for a
birthday
that suits
you.

Fashion Fiend

Party Princess

Beach Babe

AUGUST

Famous Birthday Girls

3	Martha Stewart
6	Lucille Ball
9	Whitney Houston
14	Halle Berry
15	Julia Child
16	Madonna
19	Coco Chanel
28	Shania Twain
29	Ingrid Bergman
30	Cameron Diaz

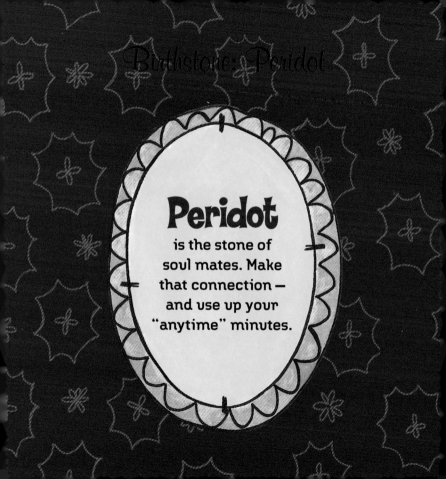

Birthstone: Peridot

Peridot

is the stone of
soul mates. Make
that connection —
and use up your
"anytime" minutes.

Remember,
you are what you eat.

(No wonder you're so sweet!)

Birthday Food Groups Pyramid

PIE

CAKE

SNACKS

ICE CREAM

COOKIES CANDY

CHOCOLATE

Character contributes to beauty.

—Jacqueline Bisset, English actress

(I guess that makes you a supermodel!)

SEPTEMBER

Famous Birthday Girls

1   Gloria Estefan

1   Lily Tomlin

4   Beyoncé Knowles

5   Raquel Welch

7   Queen Elizabeth I

15   Agatha Christie

21   Faith Hill

20   Sophia Loren

26   Serena Williams

28   Gwyneth Paltrow

Birthstone: Sapphire

Sapphire
symbolizes material wealth.
Invest wisely and you will
attract interest!

BIRTHDAY MANTRA

I'm really pretty.

No one is prettier than me.

And if they are,

Who cares? It's not their birthday.

OCTOBER

Famous Birthday Girls

1   Julie Andrews
2   Donna Karan
3   Gwen Stefani
5   Kate Winslet
8   Sigourney Weaver
21   Judge Judy Sheindlin
22   Catherine Deneuve
26   Hillary Rodham Clinton
27   Kelly Osbourne
30   Grace Slick

Birthstone: Moonstone

Moonstone

is the stone of deep
friendship, showing that you
are surrounded by love and
support. Call your best
friend and make a lunch
date for next week.

great hair

a date with
Tom Cruise

a house-
trained
puppy

world
peace

Make a wish
for the important
things in life

(one for every candle on your cake).

NOVEMBER

Famous Birthday Girls

3	Roseanne
6	Sally Field
7	Marie Curie
8	Bonnie Raitt
11	Demi Moore
15	Georgia O'Keeffe
19	Indira Gandhi
21	Goldie Hawn
25	Christina Applegate
28	Anna Nicole Smith

Birthstone: Citrine

Citrine

sparkles with success.
Let your achievements
illuminate the
autumn night.

THINGS YOU CAN ASK ONLY ON YOUR BIRTHDAY

1 Could I be any cuter?

2 Can I borrow your favorite shoes?

3 What's the most expensive thing on the menu?

Do you think 4 he likes me?

5 But seriously, could I be any cuter?

DECEMBER
Famous Birthday Girls

1   Bette Midler
2   Britney Spears
3   Julianne Moore
4   Tyra Banks
10 Emily Dickinson
18 Christina Aguilera
19 Alyssa Milano
21 Jane Fonda
24 Ava Gardner
29 Mary Tyler Moore

Birthstone: Turquoise

Turquoise
ties you into social
matters. Step out
with your friends
and celebrate!

Be your own

secret admirer.

Coming Your Way:

AN AWESOME YEAR

Hugs & Kisses

All your birthday wishes

Age doesn't matter unless you're a cheese.

—John Paul Getty,
U.S. oil magnate

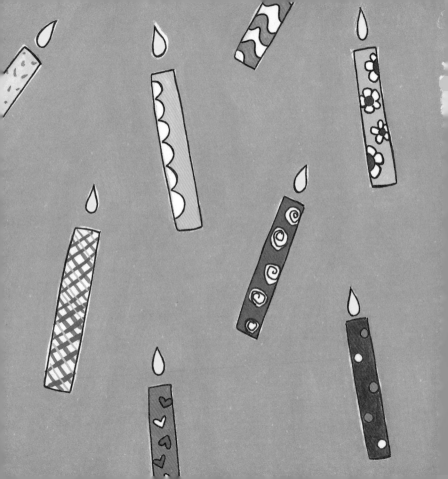